Broken Bones

There may be times when you feel broken, but it is in those times when you will achieve the most growth. And when you have healed, you will realise that you are even stronger than you were before.

Contents

Lust - 5

Foe - 29

Magic - 53

Kind - 75

The belief that others can save you.

LUST

Lust is a representation of the blights

that come with searching for love.

The rights and the wrongs that in turn make us strong.

The lessons we learn and the heartaches we face.

The acceptance that alone can be a warm embrace.

The knowledge that finding someone will never be above,

the feeling you have when you gain self love.

I am never going to restrain someone,

just because I love them.

I will never claim someone as mine.

In time I have learned how to let something be.

Trust and acceptance to let someone be free.

Hopeless and hopeful little creature,

you feature all the beauty of this world.

Hold tight in the night when you choke yourself to sleep.

Those tired eyes they weep.

Sleep.

For your love was but an inch deep.

The tremble of my lips,
the shake of my hand,
the heartbeat in my stomach.
Once again I am at your mercy.
I can't take part.
I must heal my heart.
Let me leave,
stop this love before I start it.

You are complete without another.
Love does not make you whole.
Alone does not mean lonely.
Lost does not mean no control.

Unwind in the breath of another,
the uncharted depths of a lover.
Find the time to take,
give yourself a break.
Remembering you come before any other.

Hang me in your presence,

It is your essence that I crave.

Make me your slave.

My consent I have gave.

Now I must behave to appease you.

Break my heart one more time,

    let me feel you are mine.

        You devil,

    the power that you hold.

Let me feel the pain foretold.

        Break me.

Feel the hand that takes your face
and traces down your lips.
Feel him as you kiss,
watch him as he drips.
Slowly feel him slip.
Control him,
unfold him,
and finally, just hold him.

Effective past
it lasts an eternity
I cannot yet grasp
my escape.

Lust is curious,

desperate and wanting.

It is a confronting need to be whole.

But once the moment has past,

an empty feeling lasts.

And you ask yourself if it satisfied your

goal.

If only love could fill the pain of rejection.

There is one exception.

The love you give to yourself.

When you kiss me I feel your frustration.

I'm wanting to feel your love

not desperation.

I'm looking for your heart,

not the part you want inside me.

I want it to pull you apart

to have to say goodbye to me.

If you're leaving,

just be sure,

you don't want me anymore.

For when you leave,

I shall break,

and my love for you

is what you'll take.

And in the end
she did not cry.
The silence of loneliness
was her goodbye.

Give me the strength to smile
when my heart feels weak
and tears stream down my cheek.
When my throat is so dry
I can no longer speak.
Give me the strength to smile
and remind me pain is temporary.
Give me empathy so I won't resent those
who broke me.

I thought I had a broken bone,
but I realised it was just a crack.
Is my suffering still enough
to bring your love back?

Call it loneliness or love,

but it's bringing me down to my knees.

So I pray and hope for better days.

Tonight I am longing for a taste of your affection.

I fear rejection.

Your indifference is demeaning.

This love to me has meaning.

I am beyond feeling hope,

but I can no longer cope,

pretending my heart isn't yours for the stealing.

I am not in love with him,
but I will never forget loving him.

Your broken bones have failed me.

Derailed me.

Turned me into something I'm not.

This lonely heart is aching.

Breaking.

Accepting it is lost.

Maybe just forgot.

The rabbit hole of fairy tales,
as enticing as they seem.
Are more fantasy than reality,
don't stay lost within a dream.

The enemy within yourself.

FOE

Broken bone.

Stronger than before.

Stronger due to the tears on the floor.

The crushing sensation of falling onto stone.

Alone I sit with my broken bone.

Created in a pain,

I claim as my own.

Do you know how to treat your eyes,

    that only know cries.

The tears are the fears that you hold.

Be bold, but be gentle when your thoughts are against you.

    From this pain, someone greater shall unfold.

Steady hands, for a steady heart.

She walks along a steady path.

Does this lead her to certainty?

No.

For in this journey she has far to go.

Home, alone, angry and restrained
I want to use what I have gained.
But I am pained.
Aspirations to be better begin to fade.
I am ashamed, but I cannot control my rage.
Once more I am home and in pain.

If there is a time of peace,

it is chaos that I seek.

My mind is restless in the silence.

It wants to hurt,

it needs the violence.

For when it is quiet,

the true challenge begins.

The one where I face myself and my sins.

In times of need,

I feel greed.

Believed I am owed for my pain.

I do not gain from that state of mind,

only take from those who are kind.

The monsters that lived under my bed,

grew up and moved inside my head.

My mind is black,

my eyes are dull,

my thoughts are faulted.

I am faulted.

I am breaking.

Watch me break.

My mind is light,

My eyes are bright,

My thoughts are stable.

I am stable.

I am okay.

Watch me be fine.

Have awareness of your pride.

It can eat you alive.

Those vengeful thoughts will harm you,

more than those around you.

Those unkind words you throw,

will have nowhere else to go,

but inside you is where they shall fester.

My mind has become my enemy,
and I'm needing that to end.
I'm exhausted from trying to become my own
friend.

When I ask her to be kind to me
I'm met with self-loathing.
A fear of myself has caused my imploding.

I decide to ignore her until she is better.
Realising later it was me who upset her
I ignored her needs, her wants, and desires.
Gave her no love until it was required.
Spoke poorly to her, gave her no praise.
Scolding her mistakes for hours and days.

Now a friendship has been forged,
because I started hearing
the pain she was in
is slowly disappearing.

Do you ever hear voices that are somehow both you and another?
They break you down in competition with each other.
Like an angel and a devil, they battle for your mind.
So fearsome that they turn unkind.
Are you aware of those voices?
You are more than your thoughts.
That chatter inside you
does not define you.
Rise above those thoughts that make you lost.

Those voices they run deep
for when I sleep I cannot keep my
thoughts down.
Hound me until I scream.
Finally, I find my feet,
and journey into the darkness.

The path is long,
the trail is broken.
Please take my fear
as a passing token.

I need to distract myself from my mind,
when the world is silent I want to cry.
My thoughts become louder and I cower in fear.
I am searching for my true voice,
the one that rings clear.

I am working

to always staying busy.

How can I think,

always staying busy.

How can I sleep,

always staying busy.

I have no time to weep,

always staying busy.

In the end, I choose to stay busy.

Healed wounds on the fourth of June,

all too soon they reopen.

Repeatedly broken,

without a single word spoken.

Hope can be a devil sometimes.

Along this journey, I've had thoughts,

of broken stones and rocks.

Fragmented and forgot.

Never returning to be whole again,

but still complete,

are they not?

What am I seeking,

what do I want to find?

Each time I think I have tamed my mind,

gained control of my life,

I am wrong.

I am constantly searching for where I belong,

Instead of just being here.

The present is where I have nothing to fear.

It is freedom that I seek.

When days start to feel longer than weeks.

When I dread the rise of the sun.

I know not who I am, but who I've become.

That someone terrifies me.

Knowing she is trapped and may never be free.

I feel almost helpless.
Maybe life has been to kind.
Now I'm waiting for the other shoe to drop.
I fear those thoughts as they create my reality.
I need to change my mindset once again.

Over-thinking has always been a cause
of sadness for me.
Maybe I need to learn to let things be.
Live in the present and not in my head.
Go with the flow and be natural instead.

Some days there are clouds,

and I feel empty inside.

But all days are blessed.

The ones tried and untried are equal.

It's okay to rest.

The transformation of your mind.

MAGIC

Sometimes I feel I don't know myself at all.
I sit and I wait and I watch myself fall.
I don't know my patterns.
I don't know my heart.
I don't know my right from wrong,
or my finish from my start.
But I do know I am strong
and I will keep myself going.
I do know I'm okay with forever not knowing.

There is a time for darkness,

if only to reveal the light.

What is a peaceful day,

without a lonesome night.

What is a long winter,

without the anticipation of spring.

What is a journey taken,

if one chooses not to begin.

Achieve what you want in a lifetime,

in just a single year.

The fear that is holding you down

will only disappear.

Be calm, but not complacent.

Find courage, seek your truth.

Only you create the life in front of you.

Tell me something about magic.

I can see it in your words and in your actions.

It is in your successes and mishappens.

Your conscious thoughts are what guide you.

Find you.

This magic is yours if you'll have it.

I am seeking a path toward healing,
asking forgiveness for the anger I'm feeling.
I'm letting go of the past,
moving forward at last,
with understanding
and compassion of past dealings.

Life is a never ending journey of good and bad.
Eternal happiness lost on those who seek it.
In a moment it could all fall.
Wondering and wandering once again to find it all.

Like a flower I am pure,
Like a river I am sure,
Like a mountain I stand tall,
Like a tree sometimes I fall.
Like an ocean I am vast,
Like a season I won't last.
But while I'm here I will grow and have no regrets when it's my time to go.

I am easily frightened,
but I pretend I am brave.
I pretend I am a warrior,
not a damsel to be saved.
Sometimes I wonder why I need to seem strong.
Why is weakness viewed as wrong?
I think its okay to be vulnerable.

How can we know of the journeys we will take.
The paths that are strong and the paths that shall break.
I am content living in the unknown.
As long as I am brave enough to stray from my home,
and learn to be alone.
Be confident enough to stand on my own.
For me, that is a life worth living.

It is peaceful being alone.

Taking note of the world from your home.

A quiet calm.

In this stillness I breathe freely.

I see who I am, and I see who I could be.

The present does not last,

it is the past all too soon.

Moments become memories,

like the sun becomes the moon.

Years aren't as long as they use to be.
Days end before they begin.
Fairy tales become stories,
In which the princess does not win.
Nights can still be scary, afraid of being alone.
Homesickness is being away from someone you love,
more than being away from your home.
Growing up is a journey,
but everyone has their own path.
Some are destined to cross just once,
while others are destined to last.

I am seeking to be free.
Rid all of my belongings, just me.
I seek to greet the day in peace,
no resistance needed.
For the day is my own,
and my life is my home,
and all I need to do is just be.

All for those brief moments of sun,

chance encounters flounder with each day begun.

Surrounded by the same, I do not change.

Remembering how to grow

is in pain.

New things are scary,

but they are also an opportunity for growth.

And I want to grow.

So for now I will embrace this fear, no matter how

uncomfortable it makes me.

Until I am no longer afraid.

Always looking for a feeling,

happiness, contentment, and passion.

These feelings are what give us meaning.

A reason for being.

But even in their absence,

life continues to grow.

And the ending of each moment

is how we can know.

When I open myself up,

not out of fear or desperation,

but pure honesty.

I seem to find what I seek.

Stand tall if you fall,

your legs are still beneath you.

Don't wallow on the floor of your failures.

Walk strong when you're wrong,

accept you're still learning.

Journey on until you know where you are going.

I have no desire to write...
I stay outside day and night.
Here I see only the present.
It is sacred to me.
Life. To be lived.
To be passionately absorbed.

When you're done living your life for
everyone else, come home.
Not to the place,
but the feeling of peace.

The love you give to yourself.

KIND

Be gentle.

Be kind.

To your body and your mind.

Take time to be grateful to your self.

Let yourself grow in thoughts of love and

forgo any hurt that you think you deserve.

Better off than I was before.
Each day and long night
reminds me of my growth,
and my newfound ability
to embrace change,
and stay true to who I am.
In the uncomfortable progress
I can see I'm doing better.

More than a life of envy,
give me a life of peace,
of fortune in the form of love.
And happiness which can be shared.
Dark times may come,
but light is a certainty.
So long as you keep your eyes open.

I am brave,

I am bright,

I find peace within the night.

Protected by my light,

I move with clear sight,

To a path that feels right.

Gentle hands for a gentle heart,
can I lead myself towards a gentle start.
Can I let go of stress and worry?
Stay motivated, find passion,
be strong, and not hurry.

Just for this moment I choose to be kind
to my body and my mind that protect me.
I choose to see my best qualities
and change those that no longer reflect me.

Can you feel the lightness of your soul,

the clean air that you hold.

The sunlight in the morning

signifying a new day dawning.

All the freedom that comes with that time.

Take in each moment you can find.

I am cultivating feelings of gratitude,
kindness, tranquility, and resolve.
With patience sustainability and mindfulness
involved.
Cleanliness and moderation are what I'm seeking.
Honest words and silent thoughts are what I am
speaking.

Every deep breath brings me a feeling of joy.
The expansion of my lungs brings me peace.
I am looking for that feeling in every action I take.
Aware of each moment I make.

Happiness can be found in simplicity.

You don't need things to be complete.

The social milestones you need to tick off,

should all be forgot.

Just be.

It takes but a second to become aware of your breath, and the present that each breath can give.

Mostly I am grateful for this feeling of ease.
Grounded like a mountain,
but changing like a breeze.
This feeling is temporary,
so I'll cherish it while it's here,
and be grateful for this peaceful moment,
even when it disappears.

I feel light in my thoughts,
my actions are slow,
I flow with unguided direction.

Wonderful human,

creating your life,

facing the strife that binds you.

You find your way in the dark

an incredible feat.

You are beyond belief

my human.

Patience in each step I take

knowing I will find sure footing.

Without looking I move,

calm and confident with the choices I make.

If I stumble I must learn to walk again.

Certain.

I take one more step.

Honeysuckle dreams,

warm winter nights,

eternal beauty fading out of sight.

Midnight rain,

gentle days,

gazing through the morning rays.

Sleepless nights that give you power,

breathing in the witching hour.

Small moments containing the beauty of the world.

Hold them close,

let the unfold.

Be gentle on yourself
the strict nature you follow
will only cause you harm
briefly productive
life lacking charm
too hard on yourself
it's okay to move slow
have patience
you will be where you need to go.

There is a cure for all your needs

and you will not find it outside you.

You cannot buy it,

but simply try it,

Breathe in,

and let it all go.

I am grateful for my life,
for the day and for the night,
for the love I give and receive,
for the joy I want to feed.
For the morning air so clean,
for my goals, hidden and seen.
For the people good and bad,
for the times both happy and sad.
I am grateful to be alive.
So while I'm here I'll do more than survive.

Be brave,

be bold,

be gentle and kind.

Protect you body,

Love your mind.

For those broken and healing.

Lightning Source UK Ltd.
Milton Keynes UK
UKHW021259071020
371168UK00010B/393